Enjoy Playing Guitar

Tutor Book 2

Next steps in playing classical guitar

Debbie Cracknell

MUSIC DEPARTMENT

OXFORD
UNIVERSITY PRESS

OXFORD
UNIVERSITY PRESS

Great Clarendon Street, Oxford OX2 6DP, England

Oxford University Press is a department of the University of Oxford.
It furthers the University's aim of excellence in research, scholarship,
and education by publishing worldwide in

Oxford New York
Auckland Cape Town Hong Kong Karachi
Kuala Lumpur Madrid Melbourne Mexico City Nairobi
New Delhi Shanghai Taipei Toronto

With offices in

Argentina Austria Brazil Chile Czech Republic France Greece
Guatemala Hungary Italy Japan Poland Portugal Singapore
South Korea Switzerland Thailand Turkey Ukraine Vietnam

Oxford is a registered trade mark of Oxford University Press
in the UK and in certain other countries

15

ISBN 978-0-19-338140-7

Music and text origination by Julia Bovee
Printed in Great Britain on acid-free paper by
Halstan & Co. Ltd, Amersham, Bucks.

All pieces are original compositions or arrangements
by the author unless otherwise stated.

Preface

Welcome to this revised edition of Book 2 from the series *Enjoy Playing Guitar*. Updated with new pieces and a fresh design, this book is suitable for all developing classical (or Spanish) guitarists and provides a natural follow-on to Book 1. It is designed for use with a teacher, but also encourages self-directed learning outside and during lessons. The material takes the student through more complex rhythms, keys, and time signatures, and introduces higher positions (2nd, 5th, and 7th). Techniques such as left-hand slurs, harmonics, and the barré are all presented with clear explanations and practice exercises. The book continues to develop all-round musicianship through improvisation, composition, playing by ear, and accompanying, and also introduces a new skill: transposition. Pieces have been carefully selected to encourage good solo and ensemble playing, with many well-known, popular tunes featuring alongside original compositions tailored to specific technical demands. Finally, the CD (inside the back cover) is for easy reference and enjoyment, while learning at home, and for gaining fluency. The features of Tutor Book 2 are as follows:

Pieces	• over 50 engaging and varied tunes, including traditional favourites, original compositions, and songs from stage and screen, all with helpful performance tips
	• a repertoire section at the end of the book, containing six extended pieces (solos and duets) for concert performance, all with useful study notes
Exercises	• to consolidate technical and theoretical points, and as preparation for pieces
Flexible arrangements	• chords, ostinatos, and improvisation-based accompaniment ideas for the teacher or second pupil
	• rounds for 2–4 players
	• more complex guitar accompaniments on the CD for home, school, or concert performance
CD	• recorded demos—including all solos, duets, and trios, plus the repertoire pieces (without repeats)—for listening and play-along practice
	• click-track intros of two bars (including any upbeats) for all demo tracks
	• recorded accompaniment parts, as backing tracks only
	• tuning notes on Track 1: each open string played three times, from string 1 to string 6
Quizzes	• helpful revision of music theory and guitar technique, as well as further questions for aural training, using the CD
Illustrations	• detailed drawings showing all new hand positions and other techniques
Chord Diagrams	• a one-stop guide (at the back) to chords used throughout the book, for accompanying and improvising activities

Debbie Cracknell, 2012

Quick Revision

Use this page to check notes, time signatures, etc. that have been covered in Tutor Book 1.

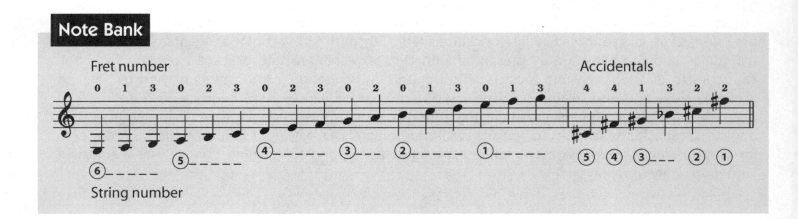

Note Bank

Fret number

String number

	Note pyramid	**Rest pyramid**

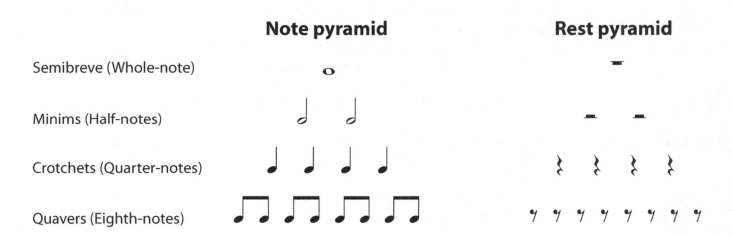

Semibreve (Whole-note)

Minims (Half-notes)

Crotchets (Quarter-notes)

Quavers (Eighth-notes)

Things to remember:

- a dot after a note or rest increases its duration by half as much again
- the semibreve rest is also used to show a whole-bar rest

Time signatures

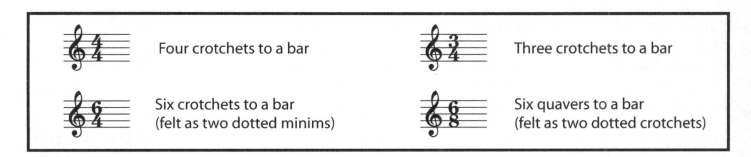

Four crotchets to a bar

Three crotchets to a bar

Six crotchets to a bar
(felt as two dotted minims)

Six quavers to a bar
(felt as two dotted crotchets)

Scales (all one octave)

G major

C major

E minor pentatonic

Introducing top A

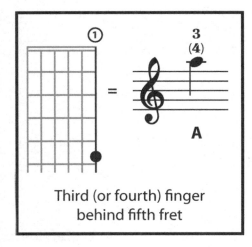

Third (or fourth) finger
behind fifth fret

You will need this A in many pieces. One of the easiest ways to reach it is to slide the third finger (or fourth, depending on the fingering of the surrounding notes) up two frets from the G on the third fret to the A on the fifth fret.

2: demo

For he's a jolly good fellow

Trad. (English)

The Pause (⌢)
This symbol above or below a note means you should hold it on for longer than usual.

The Accent (>)
This sign means that you should give the note a bit of an attack to emphasize it (strike the string with more force).

3: demo

Knights of Old

f (repeat pont.)

1., 2.

last time **Fine**

mp

mf

D.C. al Fine

mp

mp

mf

The dotted quaver and semiquaver

> The **dotted quaver** (or **dotted eighth-note**) works in the same way as the dotted crotchet (♩.), in that the dot makes the note half as long again. The dotted quaver is therefore worth three quarters of a crotchet.
>
> The **semiquaver** (or **sixteenth-note**) often follows a dotted quaver to make up one crotchet beat:

4: demo
5: accomp

(2-bar intro)

March

Accompanied

J. Küffner

f   (repeat pont.)

1.   2.

pont.   *mp*   (repeat pont.)

1.   2.

mf (nat.)*   < *f*   *mp*
pont.

* *nat.* or *naturale* means play normally, i.e. not *ponticello*

6: demo

Go, tell it on the mountain

Trad. (Spiritual)

Allegretto

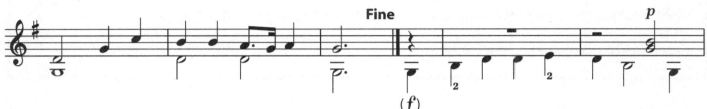

Allegretto means fairly fast and lively.

Any Dream Will Do

from *Joseph and the Amazing Technicolor® Dreamcoat*

Accompanied

7: demo
8: accomp

Tim Rice and
Andrew Lloyd Webber

(3-bar intro)

More on semiquavers

As we have seen, the note with two tails is called a **semiquaver**. It is worth half a quaver (♪) or a quarter of a crotchet (♩)

When semiquavers are written in groups of two or more, the tails are usually joined up:

A semiquaver rest looks like this:

Play the following exercises, counting as you go:

1

2

$\frac{2}{4}$ = two crotchet beats to a bar

9: demo

Drunken Sailor

Trad. (English)

'Drunken Sailor' can be accompanied with just Em and D chords (for all chords needed for accompaniments in this book, see Chord Diagrams, p. 61). Try to work out where the chords change by playing with another pupil or with the CD (track 9).

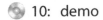 10: demo

Dance of the Fishermen

11: demo

Ring the Bell

Trad. (French)

Play 'Ring the Bell' as a round in up to four parts, with each 'voice' beginning when the previous player reaches *. You can repeat the tune as many times as you like, but all players should end at a (︵) to finish on a full chord.

Harmonics

A diamond-shaped note indicates that you should play a **harmonic**—a note with a bell-like sound, which can be an interesting effect in certain pieces of music. To produce a harmonic, touch the string lightly at the twelfth fret with a left-hand finger (directly above the fret, not behind it) and pluck with the right hand, using free strokes. You should hear a bell-like note, an octave higher than the open string. Different harmonics can be found at the seventh and fifth frets.

Play the following accompaniment to 'Ring the Bell' using twelfth-fret harmonics on strings 2 and 3:

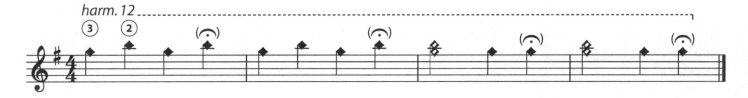

🔘 12: demo

Rocking Carol

Trad. (Czech)

Duet

Tranquillo means calmly or gently.

Allegretto Scherzoso

🔘 13: demo
🔘 14: accomp

(adapted from Op. 74, originally for flute and guitar)

Accompanied

M. Giuliani

(2-bar intro)

Scherzoso means playfully.

The suggested fingering in the first full bar and in bar 7 will keep the melody sounding smooth.

The Italian guitarists Giuliani and Carcassi wrote a great many pieces for the instrument, including both concert pieces and shorter pieces for students. Other famous composers of guitar music found in this book are Carulli (also Italian) and the Spanish composers Sor, Aguado, and Tárrega.

15: demo

Allegretto

M. Carcassi

Gretto Alle

'Allegretto' and 'Gretto Alle' can be played at the same time to form a duet, as on track 16.

Two new accidentals

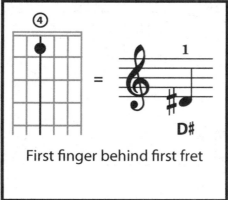

E harmonic minor scale

Remember that the F♯ in the key signature applies to all Fs, even those on string 6.

After practising the scale, try playing 'Gondola Waltz'. Bring out the melody in the bass and play the chords quietly as an accompaniment.

17: demo

Gondola Waltz

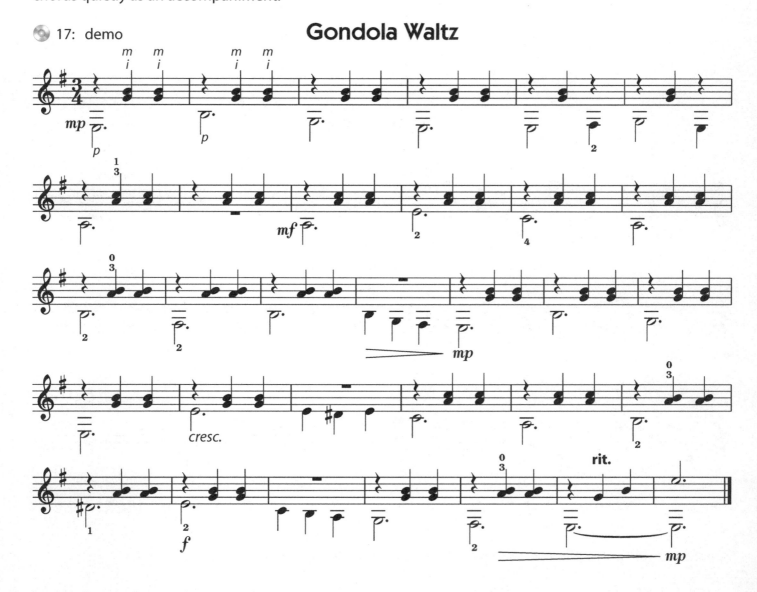

Now, playing by ear, try to work out the beginning of the famous James Bond theme, beginning on string 6 with the following:

E   F♯ F♯ F♯   F♯

18: demo

Boogie March

Moderato means 'at a moderate pace'.

19: demo

Romantic Memories

Trio

Triplets

A triplet is a group of three notes played in the time of two, indicated by a small *3* above or below the notes. So just as two normal quavers fill one crotchet beat, so do three triplet quavers.

Exercise

The following scale exercise introduces a new key, **F major**. Take note of the new key signature: in F major, all Bs are flattened. Remember, B♭ is found on the third fret on string 3.

* *simile* (or *sim.*) means continue playing in the same way, so here you should carry on playing in triplets.

In the next exercise, you'll need to take care when switching between triplets and normal quavers. Use the crotchet beat counts to help you.

This 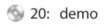 rhythm is often found in the tango, a dance from South America. Now try putting your new rhythmic skills to use in the next piece, which is an example of this dance form.

🔘 20: demo

Tango in Thirds

Duet

Two more accidentals

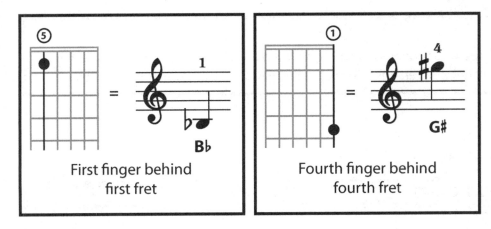

First finger behind first fret / Bb

Fourth finger behind fourth fret / G#

Before learning 'Blue Monday', try playing it as a duet, with one person playing the bass and the other playing the treble.

21: demo

Blue Monday

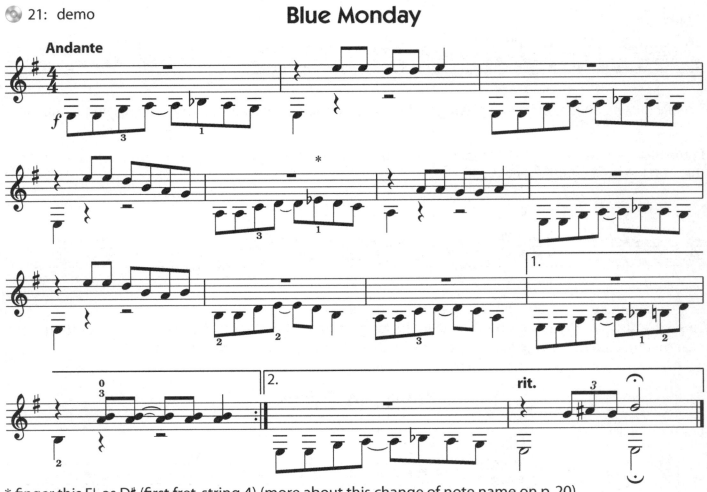

* finger this Eb as D# (first fret, string 4) (more about this change of note name on p. 20)

- You may like to improvise your own variation for the treble voice on the repeat. Use the same notes as the written piece—G, A, B, D, and E—or experiment with a **blues scale** beginning on string 4:

- 'Blue Monday' could also be played in **swing rhythm**, or 'jazz eighths'. In swing rhythm, each pair of quavers is played 'long–short', like a triplet with the first two notes tied:

Sometimes is indicated at the start of a piece. Note that on the CD (track 21) this piece is played 'straight', not in swing rhythm.

Spanish Romance

Duet

Anon.

A third guitar can add a gentle strummed chord part to 'Spanish Romance' using Am, Dm, and E chords.
Work out the order of the chords and then check that they work by playing along with track 22.

Upward slurs

A **slur** is a method of connecting two different notes together smoothly rather than playing each one separately. On the guitar, this is done using the left hand. When slurring to a higher note, play the second note by using the left-hand finger as a hammer—hit the string just behind the fret with the tip of the finger, and the higher note will sound. This technique is often called a **hammer-on**.

The slur looks similar to the tie, but remember that a tie connects two of the *same* note (leaving the second note to ring).

Exercise

* Keep holding down the C with your first finger while slurring to the D.

23: demo

Danish Round

Trad.

Play this piece as a round with each guitar starting when the previous player reaches *.

24: demo

John Peel

Trad. (English)

Duet

G.1

G.2

* **C** means 'common time' and is another way of writing $\frac{4}{4}$.

QUIZ 1

1 The printer has missed out five things in this piece of music. See if you can find all five and put them back in.

2 Tick the correct meaning:

Tranquillo =
☐ an anaesthetic
☐ gently
☐ slowly

Scherzo =
☐ playfully
☐ scarily
☐ a song

Triplet =
☐ a dance in three-time
☐ three notes played in the time of two
☐ a little fall

Hammer-on =
☐ woodwork
☐ tap the guitar
☐ an upward slur

3 Listen to 💿 track 25.

Is the tune in 2/4 time or 3/4 time? ....

Is it in a major or a minor key? ....

4 Listen to 💿 track 26. The rhythm of the tune is written on the single-line stave below. Fill in the missing rhythms in the blank bars. (You will only need to use 𝅗𝅥, 𝅘𝅥, and 𝅘𝅥 𝅘𝅥)

5 Musical sums:

If 𝅘𝅥 + 𝅘𝅥𝅘𝅥𝅘𝅥𝅘𝅥 = 𝅗𝅥 what are the following?

𝅘𝅥𝅘𝅥 + 𝅘𝅥 ....

𝅘𝅥. 𝅘𝅥 + 𝅗𝅥 ....

𝅘𝅥𝅘𝅥𝅘𝅥 + 𝅘𝅥 + 𝅘𝅥 ....

𝅘𝅥𝅘𝅥𝅘𝅥𝅘𝅥 + 𝅘𝅥 + 𝅗𝅥 ....

Big Note Bank!

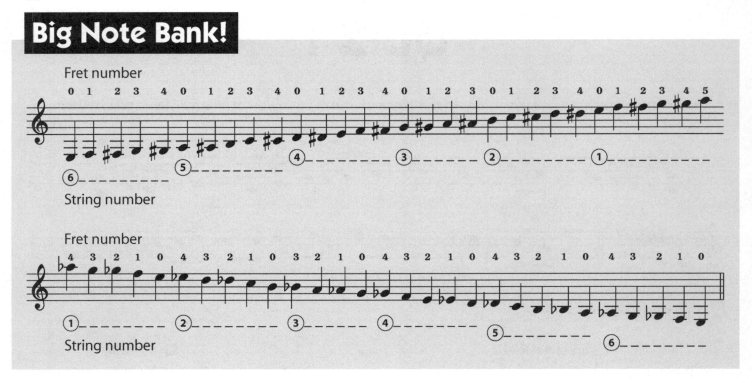

Use the Big Note Bank above to locate all the notes on the first four frets plus top A.

Enharmonics

You know that a sharp (♯) raises the pitch of a note by one fret (one semitone) and that a flat (♭) lowers the pitch by one fret.

If you look at B♭ and A♯ you will see that they are found on the same fret on the guitar; this change of name for the same note is called an **enharmonic**. See how many other enharmonics you can find using the Big Note Bank, or try working them out on your guitar.

Guitar music uses mainly sharps as accidentals but occasionally you will see a flat, B♭ being the most common. If you need to check the fingering of other flats, use the Big Note Bank above.

Chromatic scales

Chromatic scales ascend and descend one fret (one semitone) at a time. They are a very good workout for your fingers and you will often find chromatic passages in pieces of music.

Chromatic scale on G (one octave)

Now work out other chromatic scales—simply begin and end on the same letter name (either one or two octaves apart) and play all the notes in-between.

27: demo

Dark Star

Misterioso means mysteriously.

* strum with the index finger in the direction of the arrows

To produce the harmonic chord at the end of this piece, touch the first three strings with the flat of your left-hand little finger at the 12th fret and strum with the right-hand *p* or *i*.

The second position

So far, everything (except the top A on p. 5) has been in what is called 'first position', which refers to the position of your left hand on the fingerboard—in first position, your left-hand first finger plays notes on the 1st fret, the second finger (usually) on the 2nd fret, and so on. As you start to learn more complex music, you'll find that you need to move your left hand up and down the fingerboard into different positions in order to reach all the necessary notes. Different left-hand positions are indicated by Roman numerals (I, II, etc.) placed above the music at the relevant point.

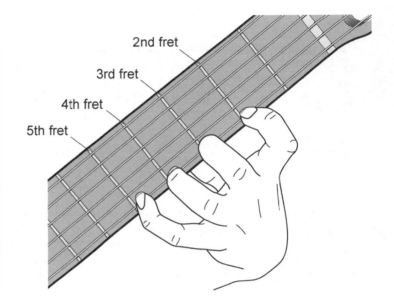

To play in second position (indicated by 'II' above the music), move your left hand up the fingerboard by one fret, so that:

finger 1 plays notes on the 2nd fret
finger 2 plays notes on the 3rd fret
finger 3 plays notes on the 4th fret
finger 4 plays notes on the 5th fret

Make sure your thumb moves up the back of the neck until it is level with the 3rd fret. Don't leave it behind!

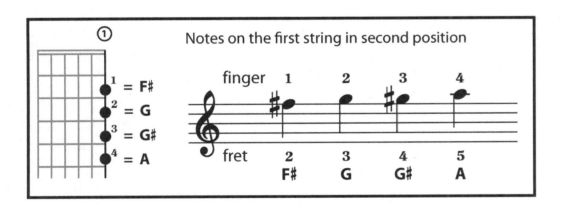

Exercise in second position

Hoedown

🔘 28: demo

In 'Hoedown', the Guitar 1 part is played in second position. Note the new key signature—both F and C are sharp throughout this piece. This new key is **D major**.

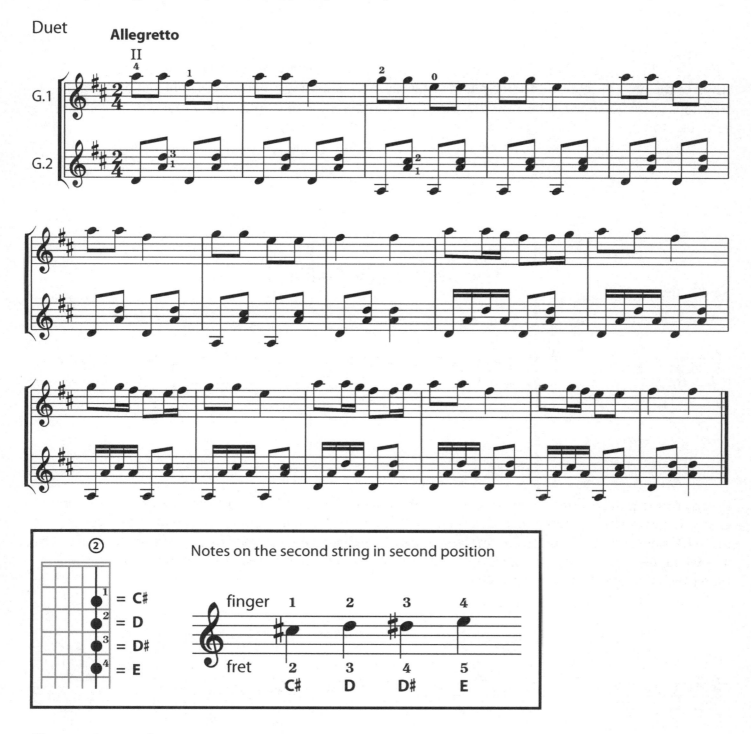

Duet

Allegretto

Chromatic exercise

Exercise in D major

* This E can be played either as an open E or as a fingered note using the fourth finger on string 2. Listen to the difference in sound between the two Es. Which has a warmer tone? There will be many occasions when you have to decide whether to use an open note or a fingered note; you may want a particular tone, or the fingering just before or after the note may help you decide.

The Sinkapace Galliard

29: demo

Melody from
William Ballet's Lute Book

In early music, players often made variations to the tune (called 'divisions') to create a longer piece. One example is given below, and is included on the CD (track 29). Try making up a second division over the given bass notes, using notes from the D major exercise above. Once you are happy with your tune, write it down in the spaces above the bass notes. Chords of D and A can be used to accompany the finished tune (the bass note indicates which chord to use).

Division 1

Division 2

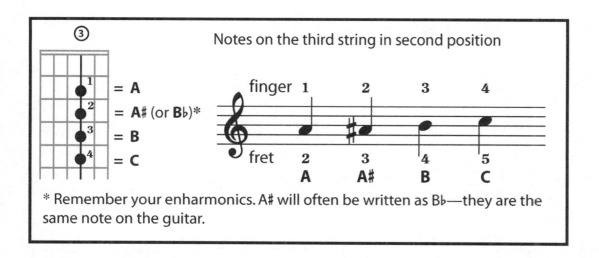

*Remember your enharmonics. A♯ will often be written as B♭—they are the same note on the guitar.

🔘 30: demo

Shaker Melody

Trad. (American)

*A dot above or below a note means you should play it **staccato** (detached). You can achieve this by deadening the note immediately with your right-hand finger or thumb. The opposite of staccato is **legato** (smooth).

A Major Scale

This new key of **A major** has three sharps in the key signature. All Fs, Cs, and Gs are sharpened.

🔘 31: demo

Little donkey

Note that the Guitar 2 part moves between first and second positions in the second section of this piece.

Eric Boswell

Practise this exercise before trying the next piece:

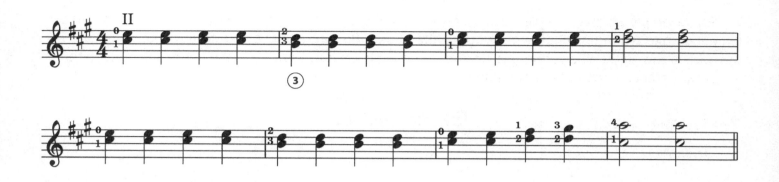

Sweet Potato

32: demo

Before playing 'Sweet Potato', try clapping the rhythms. Although written as a solo, this piece could be played by dividing the different 'voices' between two or three guitars.

First and second positions

The following pieces give you plenty of practice in moving between first and second positions. Move your left hand up to second position when you see the 'II' sign. Be sure to move your thumb along the back of the neck of the guitar when changing positions and keep the hand square to the fingerboard (keep the fingers as parallel to the frets as possible).

33: demo

Gaelic Melody

An Am chord can accompany 'Gaelic Melody'. Play **tambora**—hit the strings with the right-hand thumb, very near the bridge, while holding down the chord. Try the following rhythms:

34: demo

Jade

Duet

Now work out 'Drunken Sailor' (p. 8) in a higher key, beginning:

Note that you will need to move into second position at one point. You can accompany the tune with Am and G chords. Changing the pitch of a tune is known as **transposing**.

🔘 35: demo

In Corfu Town

Duet

Vivace means lively.

Sliding to the third position

Although not as common as other positions featured in this book, the third position is often used to reach top A (as seen in 'For he's a jolly good fellow', p. 5), and also for playing D and B together as a chord or in an arpeggio, especially when sliding to and from first and second positions. In the following exercise, when you see the 'III', simply slide your left hand up to the third fret to reach the chord.

Exercise

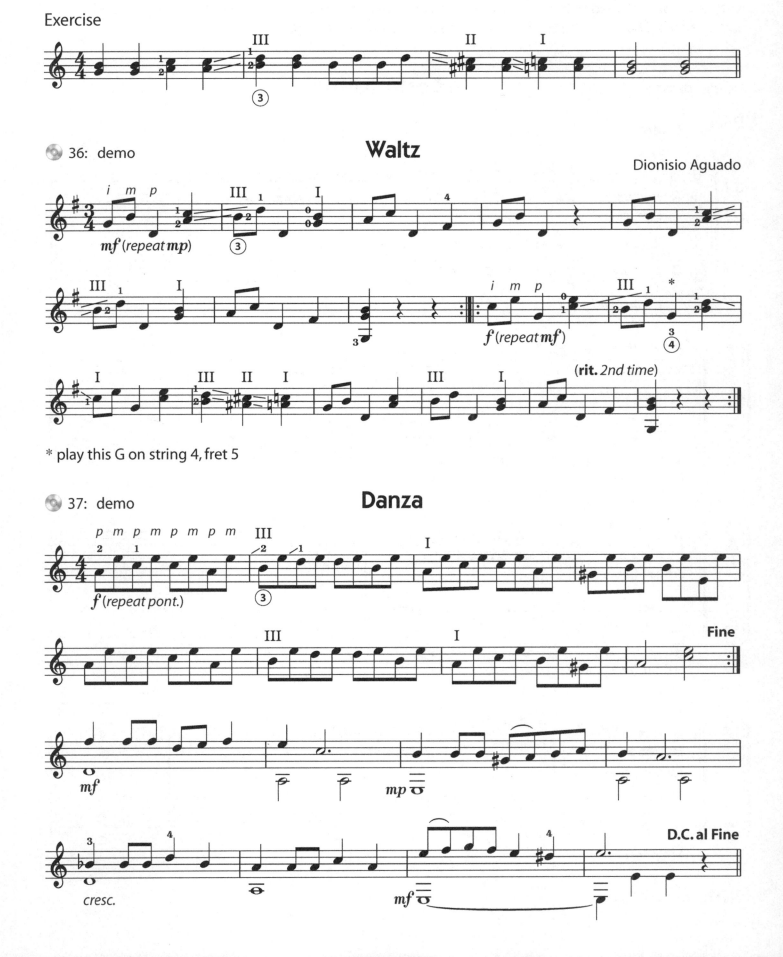

36: demo

Waltz

Dionisio Aguado

* play this G on string 4, fret 5

37: demo

Danza

QUIZ 2

1 Rearrange the letters in these anagrams. All the answers are types of music or dance.

NATOG ....
ZALWT ....
CHARM ....
SLUEB ....
GALLRIDA ....

2 Fill in the rest of the fingering of the following in second position:

3 Listen to track 38. Does it:

begin legato and end staccato ☐

or

begin staccato and end legato? ☐

4 Listen to track 39. Fill in the empty bars with the correct notes. You will only need to use ♩ beats. (The notes move by step—no big jumps.)

5 Are the notes within these pairs the same or different on the guitar?

....

The fifth position

The fifth position is very common on the guitar, with many pieces requiring you to move up the fingerboard. This book concentrates on strings 1 to 3 when not playing in first position, as these give you the notes that you will use most often. Any bass notes to be played in higher positions are indicated by the string number in a circle: ⑤

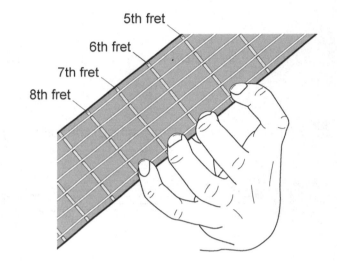

To play in fifth position (indicated by 'V' above the music), move your hand up the fingerboard so that:

finger 1 plays notes on the 5th fret
finger 2 plays notes on the 6th fret
finger 3 plays notes on the 7th fret
finger 4 plays notes on the 8th fret

Your left-hand thumb should be behind the 6th fret to balance the hand.

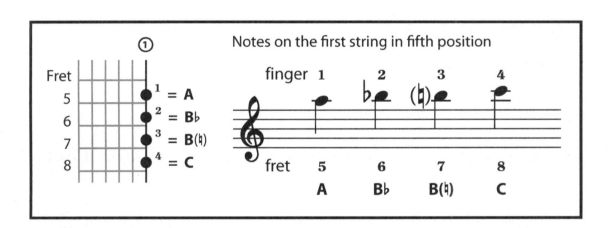

Exercise

First and fifth positions

40: demo

A Folly

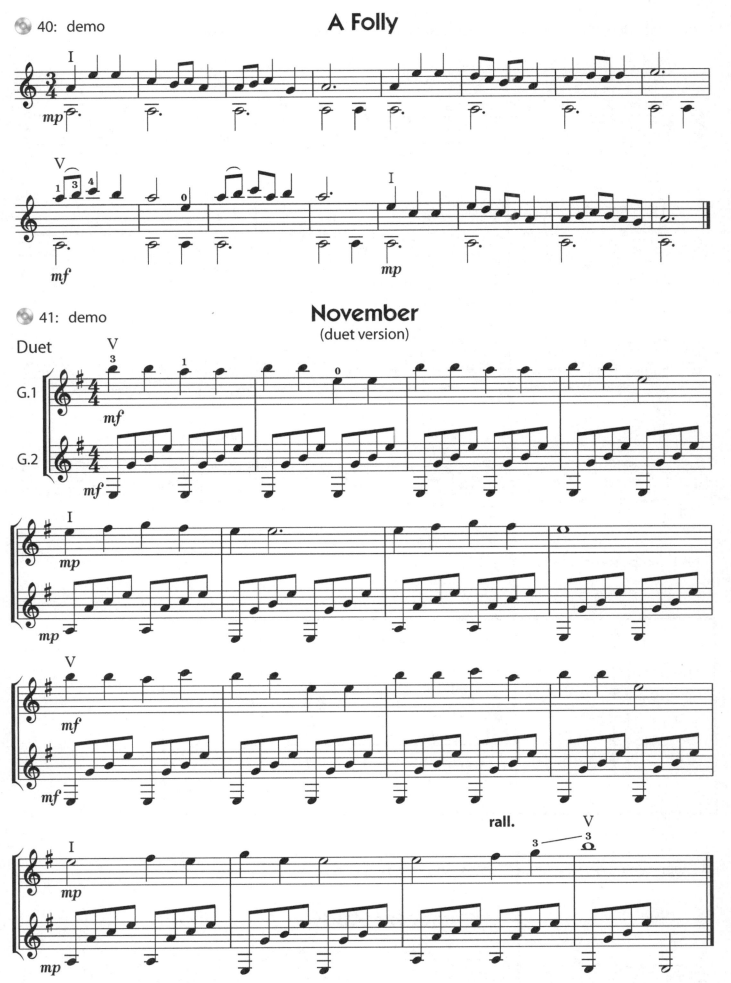

41: demo

November

(duet version)

Duet

G.1

G.2

This piece could be turned into a trio by adding gentle strummed chords of Em and Am.

42: demo

November
(solo version)

In this more difficult solo version of 'November', note the change to a triplet quaver rhythm.

* this B can be taken on string 6, fret 7

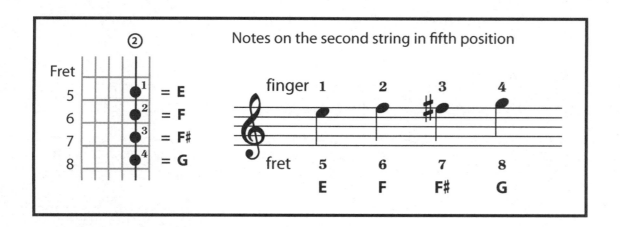

Notes on the second string in fifth position

The next study uses only 'natural' notes—no sharps or flats.

Scale Study

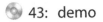 43: demo

Chorale

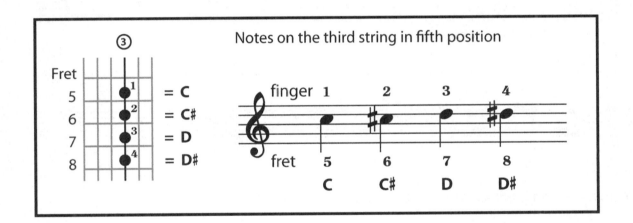

Finger aerobics!

Play through each of the following exercises two or three times, and then try them on different strings.

C Major Scale
in fifth position

Try playing the scale as a two-part round, with the second guitar beginning when the first reaches *.

Practise the C major scale before trying the next piece, 'Jason's Jig'.

44: demo

Jason's Jig

$\frac{9}{8}$ = nine quavers to a bar. This is felt as three dotted crotchets ($\downarrow$.) per bar.

When using notes that are fingered (no open strings), transposing a tune is easy—simply play in another position!

- Try shifting the C major scale up and down the fingerboard. The first note will give you the name of the scale (like the A major scale on p. 25).
- You can move 'Jason's Jig' into other positions in the same way. Once you know the fingering well, try transposing it into different keys.

The next two pieces are in the key of F major (see p. 15). Remember that in this key, all Bs are flattened. Practise the following scale exercise before playing the pieces, to get used to the B♭.

45: demo

Amazing grace

words: John Newton
melody: 19th-cent. American

'Amazing grace' gives you the opportunity to accompany with some new, more complex chords. Ask someone to play the tune while you work out the accompanying chords below, or use the recording on the CD (track 45). The Bb chord in brackets can be left out if you like—simply stay on the F chord.

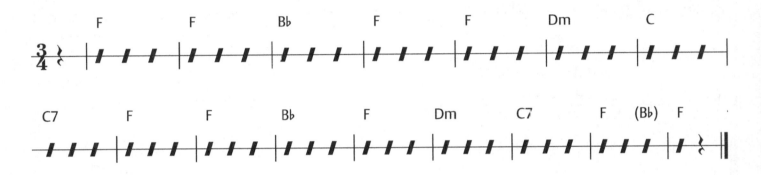

46: demo

Oh when the saints go marching in

Trad. (American)

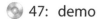 47: demo

Oxford Blues

Duet

* strum with the right-hand fingers rapidly up and down the first three strings

D.C. al Coda means repeat from the beginning to ⊕
2nd time to Coda ⊕ means jump to the Coda (the ending) the second time you reach the ⊕ sign

Guitar 1: try improvising on the repeat, for example:

etc.

Sliding into a note is also effective in blues pieces. For example, in bar 10, try playing a B (fret 7) and immediately slide to the C (fret 8).

48: demo
49: accomp

Spring

from *The Four Seasons*

Accompanied

(1-bar intro)

A. Vivaldi

* use these fingerings for smooth changes

50: demo

Tricky Tango

Trio

Downward slurs

When slurring to a *lower* note, use the left-hand finger that has just fretted the upper note to pluck the string. Use the tip of the finger—move it parallel to the fret and try to avoid twisting the hand away from the fingerboard. This technique is often called a **pull-off**.

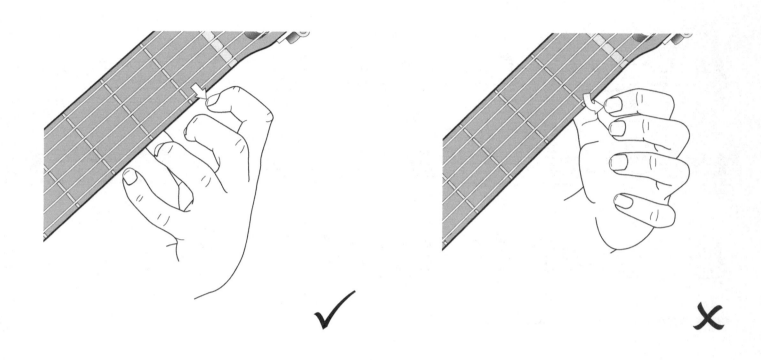

Exercises

1

2

* When slurring to another fingered note, hold down the second note very firmly to make it sound clearly.

51: demo

Waltz

Duet

F. Sor

$\frac{3}{8}$ = three quavers to a bar

52: demo

Jam on the Freeway

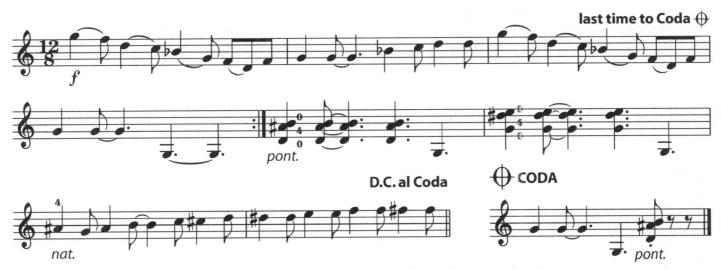

$\frac{12}{8}$ = twelve quavers to a bar. This is felt as four dotted crotchets (♩.) per bar.

Using both types of slur

The next piece, 'Los Gitanos' (which is Spanish for 'The Gypsies'), is not as difficult as it looks if you practise strumming the Dm and A chords first.

53: demo

Los Gitanos

ad lib. means 'at will', so take these passages in a free and easy manner—don't be too strict about keeping to the exact time.

a tempo means 'in time'

↑ strum these chords with the right-hand fingers in the direction of the arrow.
i m a

* *rasg.* is short for *rasgueado* (a flamenco technique) and means that you should strum across the strings with the backs of the right-hand fingernails one after the other, beginning with the little finger (*e* for *extremo*): *e – a – m – i*

The barré

Sometimes it is necessary to stop two or more strings at the same time by placing the index finger flat across the fingerboard. This is called a **barré**.

When all six strings are stopped by the index finger it is known as a **full barré** and is indicated by a C above the stave (which comes from 'ceja', the Spanish term for barré). Stopping any number of strings from two to five is referred to as a **half barré** and is shown with a ¢ (you may also see it shown as ½ C in some music, meaning the same thing).

The barré or half barré sign is usually followed by a Roman numeral to indicate which fret to use.

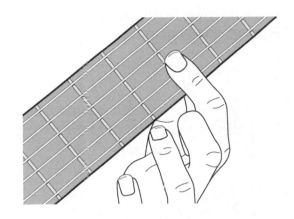

a three-string barré

The following three pieces, 'Aria', 'Packington's Pound', and 'Boulevard Barré', give you a chance to practise your two- and three-string barrés.

54: demo

Aria

* *tasto* means play near the fingerboard

🔘 55: demo

Packington's Pound

This piece uses an anonymous Elizabethan melody, originally written as a solo for the lute, an early plucked string instrument.

Duet

The Mordent (𝄘)

This sign indicates a mordent (which is optional here). A mordent is a type of ornament, which provides some decoration to the tune. Play the main note, then the note above, then return to the main note, all very quickly, using a left-hand slur. In bars 10, 12, and 16 of this piece, Guitar 1 would play the following:

Note that the ♮ above the 𝄘 means that the B is natural.

Strummed chords were often used in early music. You can add an accompanying part to 'Packington's Pound' using the chords below and some lively rhythms such as:

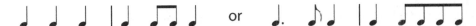

A combination of different rhythms can be effective.

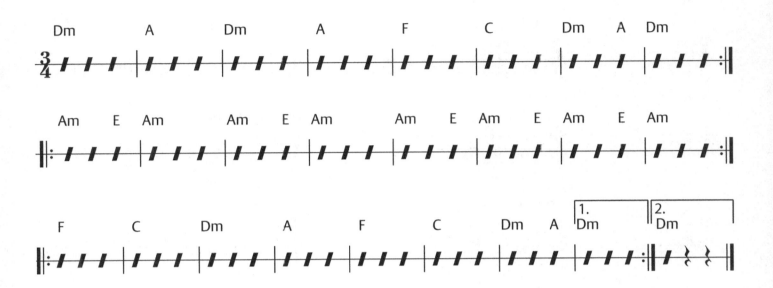

🔘 56: demo

Boulevard Barré

Repeat ad lib. and gradually fade away to nothing

Know your keys

The following keys and scales are commonly found in classical guitar music.

Keys that share the same key signature are known as **relatives**, so E minor is the relative minor of G major, and G major is the relative major of E minor (they both have F# in the key signature).

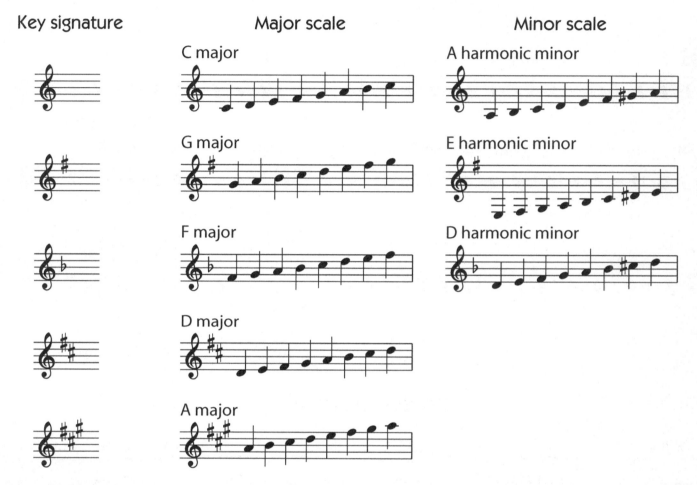

Key signature   Major scale   Minor scale

The minor scales shown are all 'harmonic' minors, where the 7th note of the scale is sharpened (with an accidental). To play 'natural' minor scales, which are found in much early music and some folk music, simply do not sharpen the 7th note. The next piece, 'God rest ye merry, gentlemen', is an example of a tune that uses the natural minor.

 57: demo ### God rest ye merry, gentlemen   Trad. (English)

Chord names are written above the tune for an optional accompaniment.

The seventh position

The seventh position (indicated by 'VII' above the music) is another very common position on the guitar. Move your hand up the fingerboard so that:

finger 1 plays notes on the 7th fret
finger 2 plays notes on the 8th fret
finger 3 plays notes on the 9th fret
finger 4 plays notes on the 10th fret

Your left-hand thumb should be behind the 8th fret to balance the hand.

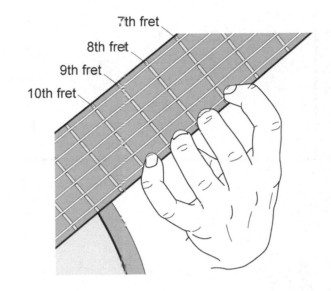

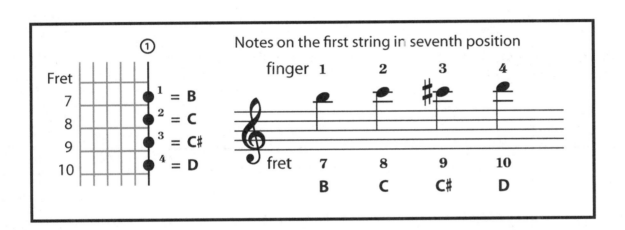

🔘 58: demo

A (Very) Little Daydream

Duet

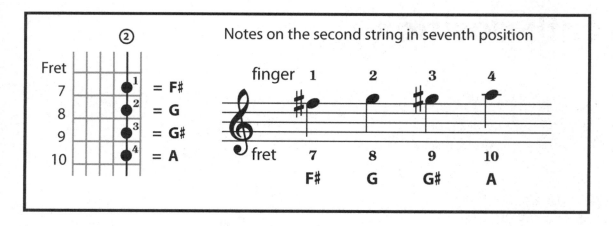

Notes on the second string in seventh position

Exercise in G major

Now try playing 'Oh when the saints go marching in' (p. 37) in the seventh position, beginning with:

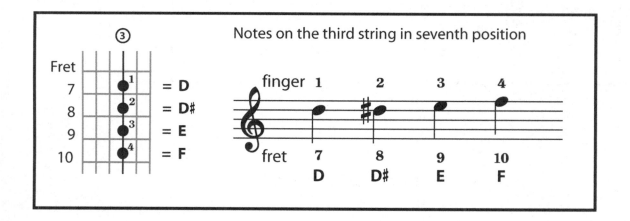

Notes on the third string in seventh position

🔘 59: demo

Tallis's Canon

T. Tallis

Play this as a round in up to four parts, with further guitars starting when the previous player reaches *. Note that the C in bar 3 is played with the third finger to allow for a smooth change.

D Major Pentatonic Scale

Pentatonic scales are often found in music from East Asia. Try improvising an oriental waltz using notes from the D major pentatonic scale above, and ask your teacher or another pupil to accompany it with the ostinato below. If you are learning in a group, take it in turns to improvise a four-bar phrase. The ostinato can also be used as a two- or four-bar introduction.

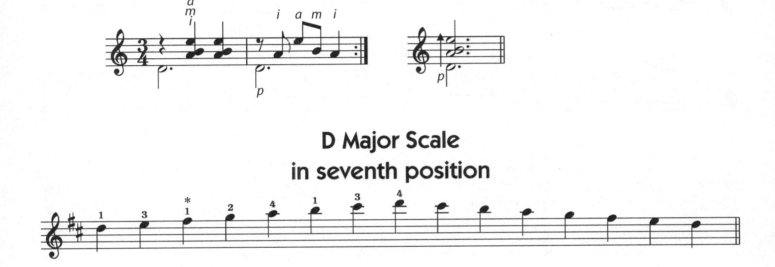

Ostinato

Finish with a strummed chord

D Major Scale
in seventh position

- This scale can be played as a two-part round, with the second guitar starting when the first reaches *.
- Note that the fingering for this scale is the same as for A major in second position (p. 25) and C major in fifth position (p. 36).

60: demo

Dara's Dance

61: demo
62: accomp

(4-bar intro)

As long as he needs me

from *Oliver!*

Accompanied

Lionel Bart

* play these Fs with the third finger to allow for a smooth change to (and from) the fourth-finger notes.

Know your Roman numerals

Guitarists need to know their Roman numerals in order to understand which position their left hand needs to be in. Use this clock face to help you learn them if they are not already familiar.

63: demo

Sundowner

This next piece features in the music to the film *Harry Potter and the Goblet of Fire*. It is played at the Yule Ball, held on Christmas Eve during the Triwizard Tournament.

Potter Waltz

Accompanied

64: demo

65: accomp

(2-bar intro)

Patrick Doyle

QUIZ 3

1 Write out these chord diagrams in stave notation. The first one is given as an example.

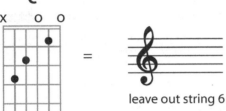

leave out strings 5 and 6

leave out string 6

2 Listen to 💿 track 66. Work out an accompanying chord part using chords A, D, and E (one per bar) and write them in the spaces given above this stave.

3 Listen to 💿 track 67.

Is the piece played **Allegro** or **Adagio**? .... Is it in 3/4 or 6/8 time? ....

4 Crossword:

ACROSS

DOWN

Six repertoire pieces with study notes

Ferdinando Carulli was an Italian guitarist and composer who wrote around four hundred works for the guitar, both solos and ensemble pieces.

In this waltz, try to bring out the melody as indicated by the accents (>). Hold the dotted crotchets (♩.) in the bass for their full value of three quaver (♪) beats.

68: demo

Waltz

F. Carulli
(1770–1841)

* *sub.* (or *subito*) means 'suddenly', so make sure you go straight back to playing quietly after getting louder through the hairpins

Ragtime music became popular at the turn of the twentieth century. Its main characteristic is the use of **syncopation**, where the tied notes throw the emphasis onto a weak beat rather than a strong one. In this piece, Guitar 1 needs to follow the fingering carefully in bars 1 and 3 to keep the melody smooth.

🔘 69: demo

Ragtime

Duet

Make sure you take this setting of the traditional folk song 'Scarborough Fair' at a steady pace—don't rush! Be careful to hold all the tied notes for their full value. Note that the C in bar 6 is played on the fifth fret on string 3.

Scarborough Fair

70: demo

Trad. (English)

Originally written for solo keyboard, this duet needs to be played at a good tempo, as indicated by the title. Keep the texture light and remember to observe the rests by damping the strings. Count bar 9 (and similar bars) carefully, with Guitar 1 following the bass note almost immediately, after the short semiquaver rest.

71: demo

Allegro

M. Clementi
(1752–1832)

'A Reflection' uses two right-hand arpeggio patterns. The pattern in bar 1 is used throughout most of the piece; the second pattern, introduced in bar 5, occurs only when there is a bass D at the beginning of the bar. Practise these right-hand patterns first on open strings. The short lines (–) above or below many of the notes indicate that you should bring these notes out to emphasize the tune.

72: demo

A Reflection

molto rall. means 'getting much slower'

Francisco Tárrega was a Spanish guitarist and composer who pioneered many of the techniques in use today on the classical guitar—notably encouraging the raising of the left leg with a footstool to support the guitar, and the development of the rest stroke.

In this piece, try to bring out the melody by emphasizing the notes on the first string (the most effective method is to use a rest stroke with finger *a* while *p*, *i*, and *m* use a free stroke—practise on open strings first). Take care to hold on to the long bass notes for their full value. A full barré is used in bar 13. Keep the finger as straight as possible and very near the fret. Don't expect a good sound straight away—it will come with practice!

Study in C

73: demo

F. Tárrega
(1852–1909)

Fingerboard fixer

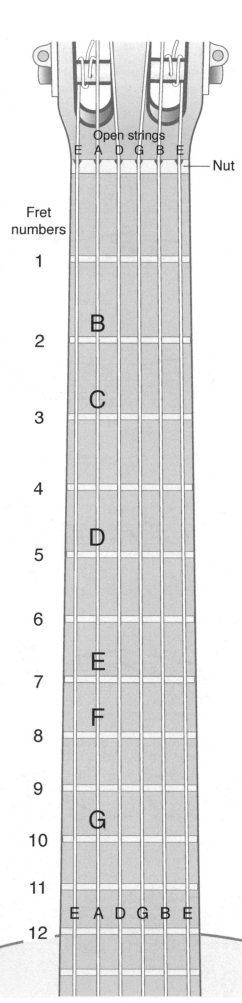

This diagram shows the guitar fingerboard up to fret 12 (where the neck and body join on a classical guitar). Fill in all the 'natural' notes—string 5 is done for you. Just remember that E/F and B/C do not have a fret separating them, as they are only a **semitone** apart. All other notes are two frets, or a **tone**, apart.

Check your answers carefully so that you then have a record of all the natural notes from fret 1 to fret 12.

Accidentals

Remember, if you need to work out a sharp (♯), just shorten the string by one fret (move your left-hand finger towards the soundhole) to make the note sound a semitone higher. For a flat (♭), lengthen the string by one fret (move towards the nut) to make the note sound a semitone lower.

Note that the 12th fret gives you the same notes as the open strings, but an octave higher.

Chord Diagrams

Chords used in Tutor Book 1:

| G | C | G7 | Am | Em | D7 | Dm | E |

  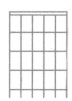 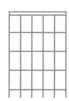 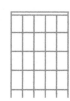 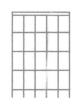

Additional chords used in this book:

| D | A | C7 | F | B♭ |

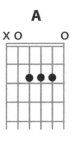 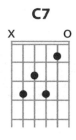   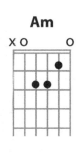 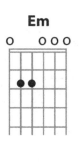 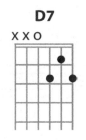 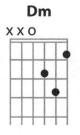 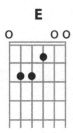 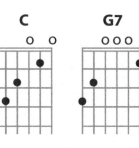

Easier versions of F and B♭:

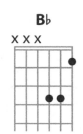

Eight chord windows for your/your teacher's chords:

Manuscript

Practice Register

Date

Date
